# TWITTER
## SAFETY AND PRIVACY
## A GUIDE TO MICROBLOGGING

**SUSAN HENNEBERG**

rosen publishing's
**rosen
central®**

New York

Published in 2014 by The Rosen Publishing Group, Inc.
29 East 21st Street, New York, NY 10010

**Library of Congress Cataloging-in-Publication Data**

Henneberg, Susan. Twitter safety and privacy: a guide to microblogging/
by Susan Henneberg.
       p. cm.—(21st century safety and privacy)
Includes bibliographical references and index.
ISBN 978-1-4488-9572-4 (library binding)—
ISBN 978-1-4488-9588-5 (pbk.)—
ISBN 978-1-4488-9589-2 (6-pack)
1. Internet—Safety measures—Juvenile literature. 2. Internet and
teenagers—Safety measures—Juvenile literature. 3. Twitter—Juvenile
literature. 4. Online social networks—United States—Juvenile literature.
I. Henneberg, Susan. II. Title.
TK5105.875.I57 H46 2014
004.67'8—d23

Manufactured in the United States of America

CPSIA Compliance Information: Batch #S13YA: For further information, contact Rosen Publishing, New York, New York,
at 1-800-237-9932.

# CONTENTS

> Twitter can be your up-to-the-minute connection to the world.

**W**elcome to Twitter! Are you excited about joining this world of 140-character tweets? Twitter is one of the simplest social media tools available today. Many teens use it for fun. On Twitter, you can keep up with your friends. You can follow your favorite celebrities. It also allows you to stay on top of the latest news and trends. And you can do this in real time! Twitter is immediate. It is about instant communication. People share, connect, and entertain each other from every corner of the world.

There are many benefits to using Twitter as a social media tool. Tweets are easy to write and read. They are sent instantly, so they are up to date. Twitter has become the go-to service when major news events are breaking. You can get your news from sources you trust. You can check Twitter on your desktop computer, laptop, or phone. Its bite-sized blogs fit in with almost everyone's lifestyle.

The use of Twitter has expanded beyond sharing communications and conversations. Twitter has had a profound effect on society. It has changed the lives of people caught in natural disasters and revolutions. From earthquake-ravaged Haiti to war-torn Egypt, Twitter has provided critical news, links, photos, and videos.

However, many of the advantages of Twitter also make it dangerous for an unsuspecting teen. Unlike your profile on Instagram, Tumblr, or Facebook, your profile on Twitter is public. So are all your tweets, unless you make them private. It is easy to embarrass yourself in front of the entire world. Once you publicly tweet, you lose control of your message. You can't restrict who reads your posts or where they get forwarded. You may endanger your reputation. You may become a target of phishing and spam attacks. These can jeopardize your account and your computer or phone. Even worse, you may endanger yourself as you lose your privacy.

These things do not have to happen, however. By becoming informed about the privacy and safety issues on Twitter, you can take charge. Becoming part of the "Twittersphere" can be fun, informative, and inspiring. You can begin or join conversations that will rock your world. Just make sure that you do it safely. You do not want to become another social media victim.

# CHAPTER ONE

# TWITTER: WHAT IS IT?

**W**hat do Olympic medal winner Gabrielle Douglas, singer Lady Gaga, President Barack Obama, and the Mars rover *Curiosity* all have in common? You guessed it! They are regular Twitter users. Teens have raced to adopt Twitter in record numbers. If you are at least thirteen, you, too, can use Twitter to interact with your friends. And you can learn to do it in ways that keep your safety and privacy intact.

## How Was Twitter Developed?

In 2006, three technology developers worked for a San Francisco, California, software company called Odeo. Evan Williams, Biz Stone, and Jack Dorsey built a social media tool for employees to communicate with each other. It consisted of short text messages of just 140 characters each. In an interview with the *Los Angeles Times*, Dorsey said that after some "name-storming" to think of words to describe the system, they looked in the dictionary. "We came across the word 'twitter,' and it was just perfect."

Twitter was introduced to the public in 2007. The developers took it to a conference in Austin, Texas. Everyone there wanted to use it. Twitter use then exploded. By 2009, it was the third most popular social networking site in the United States. In 2010, even the astronauts aboard the International Space Station were posting a dozen tweets per day. This was the year the little blue bird joined the logo. By the end of 2012, the company had two hundred million users around the world and saw four hundred million tweets per day, according to TechCrunch.com.

Software engineers Evan Williams, Biz Stone, and Jack Dorsey created Twitter to be a fast, fun way to communicate.

## How Does Twitter Work?

A Twitter account allows a person to send short messages. These are called tweets. A tweet is like a blog post in that

Twitter allows you to stay in touch on your smartphone, tablet, or computer.

it allows people to share content with others who have similar interests. It is like a text message in that it is very short. A tweet needs to be 140 characters or less. A user chooses to follow other users to read their tweets. The tweets appear in reverse chronological order on the user's home page. That means they are listed with the newest one first. Let's say you choose to follow twenty people. On any day, you will see a mix of tweets on your home page. As you scroll down, you might see where your

## > WHAT ARE BLOGGING AND MICROBLOGGING?

A blog is a series of written entries posted on the Web. It is like an online diary. The word "blog" is a combination of two words: Web + log. The entries are usually about one topic, such as comics or cooking. They may contain text, pictures, and links to other Web sites. Microblogging is a type of blogging with very short posts. These can be written and posted very quickly. Twitter is an example of a microblog.

friends are. You might see what your favorite celebrities are doing. You might even get a homework reminder from your math teacher.

## How Do Individuals Use Twitter?

Most people use Twitter in several ways. They give their followers updates on what they are thinking and doing. This is mostly what celebrities tweet about. Fans can connect with celebrities on a daily basis. For example, Justin Bieber, Rihanna, Lady Gaga, and Taylor Swift use Twitter to engage their fans. Olympic gymnast Gabrielle Douglas tweeted about her gold medals within hours after her award ceremonies. Basketball player LeBron James has millions of followers.

Taylor Swift takes a photo to tweet to her fans.

Early on, some celebrities and the owners of popular brand names found out that fake accounts were being created to fool users. Twitter set up a way to confirm that accounts are real. Legitimate Twitter accounts are called "verified accounts." Users can check to see if an account is real by going to its profile page. There they can look for a verified account badge (an icon with a white check mark on a blue background) near the username.

Twitter users can also hold conversations with their friends and people they meet on Twitter. These conversations are about the interests they have in common. For example, many users followed athletes who competed in the 2012 London Olympics. They also chatted among themselves about the athletes' performances. On Twitter, teens can find other teens who share their interest in music, books, sports, or animals. They can discuss veganism, zombie movies, or thousands of other topics. Twitter users share photos, videos, and links they find interesting. They also pass along tweets they like, called retweets (RTs).

Many people use Twitter to keep up with breaking news. Because tweets are posted instantly, Twitter followers sometimes find out about events before the news media does. This has happened during natural disasters, political revolutions, and sporting events.

A 2012 survey by BusinessInsider.com found that 28 percent of teens ages thirteen to seventeen sometimes use Twitter, and 11 percent use it each day. The biggest group of users is young adults ages eighteen to twenty-nine. Over half of all users access Twitter from their cell phones. Twitter use continues to grow rapidly each year.

## How Do Organizations Use Twitter?

Businesses, political parties, and organizations all use Twitter. Business owners use it to promote themselves to followers. For example, Zappos.com encourages its employees to tweet about new products. You can do a search for all your favorite consumer items on Twitter. If you follow a company, you might receive information about the latest products. You might also hear about sales and discounts.

During political campaigns, political parties send out tweets about their candidates. President Barack Obama was one of the first presidential candidates to use Twitter.

His campaign used it to announce rallies and answer questions. Obama also used Twitter to announce victory and thank supporters in 2008 and 2012. Many other elected officials tweet about what they are doing to serve their constituents.

Organizations use Twitter to share news. They can publicize their events and raise money. They can quickly call attention to issues. They can also send links to people or corporations that might want to offer financial support. Members of organizations can find each other on Twitter. They can share their ideas about the organization.

There are numerous examples of "networked nonprofits." These are organizations that use social media in their work for the public good. For example, followers of the American Red Cross find out about floods, hurricanes, and other natural disasters on Twitter. They also receive reminders to learn to swim or tips on how to stay cool on dangerously hot days.

Learning about Twitter is easy and fun, and it can open up a whole new world of social media. Since its development in 2006, Twitter has attracted millions of users. You can be one of them. Taking the time to learn about using Twitter safely can pay off in hours of enjoyment.

# SETTING UP A SAFE ACCOUNT

# CHAPTER TWO

**I**f you have decided to join Twitter, signing up is easy. First, though, you need to check with your parents. They may have concerns about your safety and privacy on Twitter. Those concerns are real. Make sure you follow the guidelines in this book.

You need to be thirteen or older to open a Twitter account. This rule comes from the Children's Online Privacy Protection Act (COPPA), passed by Congress in 1998. The COPPA law says that children under age thirteen must have parental consent to give personal information to a Web site. You do not need your parents' consent to have a Twitter account if you are over thirteen. However, your parents need to know if you are signing up for any account that is open to the public.

It is easy to see that some people under thirteen have Twitter accounts. This is not a good idea. Many tweens and younger teens do not have the maturity to handle a social media site like Twitter. Often they post personal items without thinking about it. Later they come to regret it. At that point, it's too late. If you are under thirteen and are thinking about signing up with Twitter, hold off. You are still able to

Keeping parents involved will help teens stay safe on social media sites such as Twitter.

read others' tweets. Waiting until you are at least thirteen to have an account will save you and your parents a lot of trouble.

## Creating an Account

Begin your account at Twitter.com. You need to use your full name and an e-mail address. Your full name becomes your username, but you can change this later. Microsoft's Safety & Security Center recommends that you do not use

## > CHOOSING
## > A PASSWORD

Many teens are tempted to choose an easy password. What is the most commonly used password in the United States? You guessed it! It's the word "password"! Other common passwords are "12345," "qwerty," and "abc123." According to Time.com, in 2012, the sixth most common password was "monkey." Passwords such as these are very easy for a hacker to guess. Experts recommend against using any version of your name or even your pet's name. A strong password contains letters, numbers, and symbols. It also uses uppercase and lowercase letters. You can make it something you'll remember. For example, say your favorite baseball team is the Philadelphia Phillies. Take the word "Phillies" and write it backwards. Turn the letter "s" into a dollar sign. Change the "ph" to "f" because they sound the same. Capitalize a middle letter. Add a "7" at the end to remind you that there are seven letters. Now your password is "$eilLif7." You have a password that is very difficult to guess but that you can still remember.

your real name as a username. It recommends that you use a nickname so that you remain anonymous. Before you create the account, the site warns you that others will be able to search for you by your real name, username, or e-mail. You won't stay secret on Twitter for long.

The next step is to choose a password. You may be inclined to use the same password you use for your other accounts. But there are several reasons to create a new password. Thousands of Twitter accounts have been hacked. This means that someone illegally obtained access to the accounts. Justin Bieber and Lady Gaga are only a few of the celebrities who have been victims. When an account is hacked, the real user is no longer in control. The hacker can post whatever he or she wants. Bieber's hacker posted his phone number. Embarrassing messages were sent from singer Britney Spears's account. Fox News was hacked. Tweets came out about President Obama's supposed death. Be smart about your Twitter account. This is a great time to choose an effective password.

## Setting Up Your Profile

When you sign up for a Twitter account, you need to agree to the terms of service. These are the rules for using Twitter. You will learn more about these rules in the next sections. Then you will be asked to upload a picture to use as your avatar. It is safer—and way more cool—to use a cartoon, symbol, or icon instead of a photo. Another idea is to only use a small section of a personal photo. Your friends will be able recognize you. However, no one else will know that you are a teen.

The next step is to write a biography. You need to keep it short, as you get to use only 160 characters. What should you write? Followers are most curious about your interests. So skip where you were born and mention your hobbies and passions. Remember, your profile is public and anyone can read it. Do not give out information about where you live. Don't even mention your school or sports team. Microsoft's Safety & Security Center advises that revealing too much information can make you vulnerable to online bullying, Internet predators, Internet fraud, or identity theft. Your goal is to keep personal data private.

> Set up your Twitter profile to highlight your hobbies and interests but not your location.

## Account Settings

When you finally see your home page, take the time to make sure your account settings protect your privacy. To protect your privacy, undo some of the default settings. These are the basic settings that Twitter chooses for you. Unless you select something different, these settings take effect by default. For example, it is a good idea to change Twitter's default for resetting a password. The default setting allows you to start the process of changing your password just by entering your username. You can change this setting so that more information is required to reset your password. This makes your password more secure.

In addition, you don't want others to be able to find you by e-mail address. You also don't want location information added to your tweets. You never want to let the world know where you are. You do want to protect your tweets, or exercise control over who can see your messages. You will learn more about protecting your tweets in the next section.

Keep the default setting for the category called "Tweet media." This way, you will always be warned if tweets contain sensitive content. For example, a tweet may contain references or links to inappropriate videos or photos.

For the most protection, don't enable the "personalization" setting. Twitter is able to track your visits to any Web sites that contain a link to Twitter. It can use your Web surfing interests to suggest people to follow. However, there are privacy concerns about this practice. Twitter puts "cookies," unique identifying data, on your computer. It collects information about your Internet use. You do not have any control over how Twitter uses this information about you. It is safer to refuse to allow Twitter to do this. You will have no problem finding interesting content on Twitter without this feature.

You will have the most fun on Twitter if you don't have to worry about safeguarding your privacy. You can tweet your friends and check up on your favorite celebrities. You can find out what's going on with matters related to your hobbies and interests. You can be part of the excitement of social media. And you can stay safe.

# MYTHS AND FACTS

**MYTH:** Twitter is safe because you can remain anonymous.

**FACT:** Even if you have protected your tweets, your profile is public. Anyone can target you for cyber crime by using your avatar, biography, and location. You can use your account settings to make sure that you are truly secure and private.

**MYTH:** You can remove your tweets from the Internet any time you want.

**FACT:** Twitter is a public space. Unless you delete a tweet within a few seconds of posting it, search engines such as Google will index it. Anyone who does a search for your name in a search engine will find it. The only way to keep your tweets private is to protect them. You can also use direct messages to keep your posts among your friends and family.

**MYTH:** You can trust all the people you meet on Twitter.

**FACT:** While most people on social media sites are trustworthy, some are not. It is easy for people to lie about themselves when setting up their profiles. Use the same common sense safety rules you use for other social media. Never give out personal information. Never arrange to get together with someone you meet on Twitter without telling your parents and taking someone with you. Block any tweets that seem threatening.

# CHAPTER THREE

# TWITTER GUIDELINES AND BEST PRACTICES FOR TWEETING

**T**he last thing many Twitter users think about is their privacy. However, it should be the first thing you think about. Most of what you say on Twitter can be saved or sent on to others. And it's not just your own privacy you need to worry about. If you use your friends' names or phone numbers in a tweet, you are compromising their privacy also. So how can you safeguard privacy?

Twitter has established its own rules and best practices for maintaining privacy. Two of the company's suggestions are especially important for teens. One suggestion is that teens protect their tweets instead of making them public. Another good idea is that teens use direct messages, or DMs, to communicate with their friends. This way, they have more control over who sees the content of their tweets.

## Protecting Your Tweets

When you first open an account with Twitter, your tweets are public. This means that anyone can view them. This

Twitter can help you keep up with your friends. However, unless you protect your tweets, they are available to the entire world via Google and other search engines.

may seem exciting at first. However, these tweets are soon indexed on Google and other search engines. Anyone who searches for your name can find the tweets. You don't know when these messages, some probably sent impulsively, will come back to haunt you. It is a good idea to protect your tweets. People will have to request to follow you. And each follow request will need your approval.

When you change your public tweets to the protected setting, Twitter puts some restrictions on your tweets. No one, even those whom you have approved to see your tweets, can retweet your tweets. This means that your tweets cannot be forwarded to someone else. Protected tweets will not appear in a Twitter or Google search. Also, you cannot send a reply to anyone who isn't following you. You haven't given such people permission to see your tweets.

Many people remember the case of an impulsive tweet sent by a seventeen-year-old Kentucky girl in 2012. This was an example of the potential danger of Twitter communication. A victim of sexual assault, she tweeted the names of her attackers. This violated a court order to remain silent, since the attackers were minors. She faced legal action for making public what legally should have remained private.

## How to Protect Your Tweets

It is easy to protect your tweets. The default setting is for your tweets to be public. You need to find the "tweet privacy" section in your account settings. There, you can change your tweets from public to private. Any tweets you made before doing this, however, will stay public. Once you have protected your tweets, anyone who wants to follow you will have to request your permission.

Protecting her tweets could have saved twenty-two-year-old graduate student Connor Riley's potential job. In 2009, she tweeted about her decision to possibly accept a "fatty paycheck" at technology company Cisco while "hating the work." It didn't take Cisco long to hear about the public tweet. The job offer was withdrawn. In an interview with MSNBC.com, Riley said, "I was using [Twitter] more like I

## > KEEPING YOUR PASSWORD SECURE

Keeping your password secure is one of the most important steps in keeping your online accounts safe. Yet according to a 2011 Pew Research Center report, one-third of all teens have shared a password with someone else. For girls ages fourteen to seventeen, the number is higher—almost one-half. Teens reported that they saw password sharing as a sign of trust. Social media sites, including Twitter, warn against sharing passwords. A boyfriend or girlfriend who seems trustworthy today could turn on you tomorrow. Don't share your password with anyone. Someone who is really your friend will understand if you refuse to divulge it. And you can show your respect for your friends by never asking them to share their passwords.

was on Facebook. I was posting status updates to people who are my friends, not realizing or caring that everybody in the whole world could see my updates because I wasn't thinking my updates were interesting to anybody outside my group." This disaster could have been avoided had Riley protected her tweets.

## How to Approve or Deny Follower Requests

Friends who want to follow you on Twitter can make a request to do so. You will see the requests on your Twitter home page. You will also receive an e-mail notifying you that someone wants to follow you. When you receive these requests, you have two options. You can approve them one at a time. Or you can choose to approve all of them at once. It's better to approve each one individually. That way you will know exactly who is following you. Why is that important? According to a 2011 Pew Research Center report, 88 percent of teens that use social media have witnessed other people being mean or cruel on social networking sites. Approving only friends will help make your Twitter experience more positive.

In 2010, talk-show host Conan O'Brien randomly chose nineteen-year-old Sarah Killen to be his only Twitter user to follow. She went from three followers to twenty thousand in one week.

# Direct Messages

Another way to safeguard your Twitter account is to use direct messages. A direct message is a tweet sent to one of your followers. You can send a DM only to a Twitter user who is following you. You can receive DMs only from users you follow. You can send them to your friends to make plans for future get-togethers. You can send birthday greetings, reminders, or a tweet just to say "hi."

Sending a DM is easy. It is one of the menu items on your Twitter home page. You can also send DMs from third-party apps such as TweetDeck. One advantage of using third-party apps is that you can send the same message to more than one person.

However, it is easy to make a mistake while sending DMs. Instead of your message being private, it becomes public for everyone to read. The most famous case of a private DM becoming public is that of former New York Congressman Anthony Weiner. In 2011, he mistakenly sent an indecent photo of himself. It was intended to go to a personal friend. Instead, it became public for everyone to see. Because of his public embarrassment, he resigned from Congress.

Unfortunately, this kind of mistake happens all the time. Michael Fertik, head of Reputation.com, told the *Huffington Post* that the accidental exposure of messages meant to be private happens "millions of times a day." Olympic medalists and Hollywood actors are among those who have regretted a public message meant for private accounts. Make sure your DMs go only where they are supposed to, or you may soon find your messages all over town.

## Tips for Safe Social Media

Protecting your tweets and using direct messages are two ways to maintain a safe presence on Twitter. Here are some other suggestions for safeguarding yourself on Twitter or any social media site.

Never post personal information such as phone numbers or addresses. According to a 2012 report from BusinessInsider.com, one-third of teens have posted their cell phone numbers online. Doing this allows you to be a target for harassment. It's also dangerous to give out a home address. There have been cases in which criminals have figured out when families are on vacation and houses are empty.

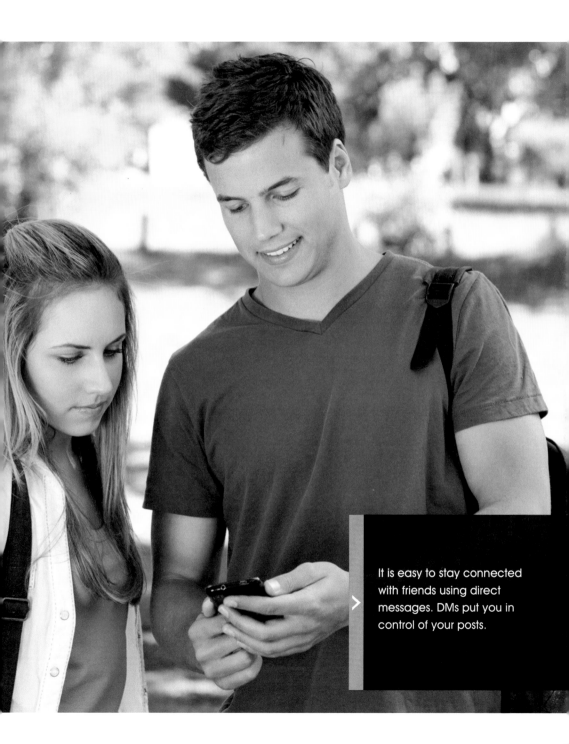

It is easy to stay connected with friends using direct messages. DMs put you in control of your posts.

Another mistake that some people make is sending credit card and banking information. Online privacy experts use the example of teens that were so excited about their new debit card that they took a picture of it and sent it to their friends. Even if you are using protected tweets or DMs, keep financial information to yourself.

Safeguard all password information. Even if you would never tweet your Twitter password, think about the security questions. If you used your mother's maiden name, the name of your pet, or even your birthday, a determined thief could figure it out.

Finally, don't enable the "tweet location" feature in your Twitter profile. If you do provide your location and you tweet that you're alone and bored, you may be inviting strangers to find you. This could be dangerous if a stranger turns out to be a predator. You are smart to provide nothing but general hints as to your whereabouts.

You can stay safe and private on Twitter and still have fun. Protecting your tweets and using DMs will allow you peace of mind and a great online reputation. There are thousands of teens and young adults right now who wish they had followed that advice. They are the ones trying to take back messages and photos that never should have been sent.

# TAKING CHARGE OF YOUR ONLINE PRESENCE ON TWITTER

# CHAPTER FOUR

**H**ave you ever searched for your name using an online search engine such as Google? If you haven't, you might be surprised or even shocked to discover what is there for everyone to see. Instant messages from middle school, silly videos posted on YouTube, and cell phone photos from a party are all items teens have been horrified to find. Once things are posted online, they are often impossible to remove. Numerous companies have been created to help social media users clean up tarnished reputations. It takes time and money to recover your good name once it has been lost. It is better to guard your reputation from the beginning of your online presence.

## Protecting Your Online Reputation

Studies show that teens do care about their online reputations. A 2011 Pew Research Center study on teens and the Internet revealed that more than half of the teens surveyed decided not to post something because it might reflect

Greek athlete Voula Papachristou lost her chance to compete because of an offensive tweet she posted during the 2012 Summer Olympics.

badly on them. According to the study, older teens in particular are aware that colleges and future employers can judge them based on online content.

The study showed that even younger teens were concerned about privacy. In a Pew Research Center focus group, a middle school boy said, "Twitter is scary because it's so much more—like you can Google my name and it will have my Twitter account." He ended up deleting his account. You need to be vigilant about your reputation. You have to think about how your posts can damage your good name in the future. And you need to worry about what other people say about you.

## Think Before You Tweet

Most online experts agree that the best advice they can give to teen tweeters is: "Think before you tweet." In 2007, Harvard researchers found that teens can be highly impulsive. They suggested that the source of impulsivity might be in the teen brain, which is not fully mature.

Firing off a tweet is fast and easy. Say you see a situation that provokes an emotion such as anger or envy. You might be tempted to tweet your friends before you have a chance to think clearly. Certainly that is what happened to several athletes in the 2012 Summer Olympics. A Swiss and a Greek athlete were expelled for sending racist tweets. Each lost the chance to earn a medal because of a thoughtless post in a moment of anger. In 2012, an inappropriate tweet sent impulsively in a school library cost a University of Nevada, Reno, student body officer his position. Here is an important rule: if you wouldn't say something to someone's face, don't put it on social media.

If you feel attacked by a tweet and are reacting emotionally, a good idea is to take a break. Leave your computer and do something fun for ten minutes. Listen to music, draw, or shoot some baskets. This allows you to gain perspective. You will respond with a calmer tone. Or you may just decide to let the attack go. This strategy may prevent you from doing something you will later regret.

Teens also need to be aware that their actions on Twitter can hurt their family. The experts at Reputation.com use the following example. A teen tweets that his father is in a bad mood. The father blames his boss at work. If this got back to the boss, the boy's dad could be in real trouble. You might want to blow off steam about your parents, teachers,

President Barack Obama interacts with citizens during "Twitter Town Hall" events.

and coaches. But word travels fast in social media. The next thing you know, the targets of your anger are coming back at you. If you need to vent your emotions, do it with trusted friends in person. If someone you follow seems to provoke you into tweets you regret later, perhaps you should stop following that person.

It is a good idea to keep track of what other Twitter users are saying about you. When someone includes your username preceded by an @ sign in a tweet, it is called a "mention." Your "mentions" tab collects the tweets so that you can see the conversations about you.

## Blocking Tweets and Unfollowing

Like other social media sites, Twitter has its share of people who make rude and inappropriate remarks. If you are receiving tweets with offensive content, Twitter provides several tools you can use. The first tool is to block the Twitter user. Blocked users cannot add your Twitter account to their lists. They can't follow you. They can't see your profile picture. However, if your tweets are public, blocked users can still read them and send replies.

Another tool you can use is to "unfollow" another user. In this case, you will no longer see that person's tweets in your home timeline. This will not stop the tweeter from posting offensive tweets. If those tweets are targeted at you, this may be bullying.

## > SUICIDE-RELATED CONTENT ON TWITTER

Some Twitter users may use Twitter to reach out for help with their painful problems. You might even come across a user who is threatening suicide. If you know the person, alert your parents or other trusted adults. With their help, you can contact the individual personally to make sure he or she is OK. Share with the user resources such as the National Suicide Prevention Lifeline (1–800–273–TALK). If you don't know the person, contact Twitter and file a report. Twitter has a form you can use on its Help Center page. Twitter representatives will reach out to the user. They will keep your name confidential. However, they will provide the user with resources and encourage him or her to seek help.

## From Online to Real World: Cyberbullying

In 2010, the Pew Research Center reported that almost one-third of teens had experienced some form of online harassment. This includes having private material forwarded without permission, receiving threatening messages, or having someone spread a rumor about them online. Teens who have been bullied or harassed online report a higher incidence of depression and ideas of suicide. They avoid school more than those who have not been bullied.

What can teens do if they have been victims of cyberbullying on Twitter? Cyberbullying is like real-world bullying. If you have become a victim, you have to tell an adult about it. Abusive behavior on Twitter is a violation of Twitter policies and terms of service. You can file a report on your abuser using an online form found in the Twitter Help Center. Twitter representatives will investigate your complaint and take action. This may lead to the closing of the abuser's Twitter account. However, with the help of parents and teachers, you will likely have to confront the cyberbully in the real world to completely stop the behavior.

Teens who use Twitter for entertainment and connection don't want to think about the negative aspects of it. But even one inappropriate tweet can cause both online and offline damage for years. The negative consequences can ruin reputations and future prospects. Taking responsibility for your Twitter posts means thinking very carefully about what you write. Protecting your tweets, monitoring your mentions, blocking abusive users, and confronting bullying are all great steps to maintaining a positive online presence.

# 10 GREAT QUESTIONS

## TO ASK AN INTERNET SECURITY EXPERT

**1** Why should a teen without a credit card worry about identity theft from a Twitter account?

**2** What should I do if I'm being bullied through my Twitter account?

**3** What should I do if I accidently get a virus on my computer through my Twitter account?

**4** Why do I get phishing attempts from my friends' Twitter accounts?

**5** What do I do if someone sends a threatening tweet to me?

**6** How can I protect my Twitter account if I lose my phone?

**7** How can I tell if Twitter apps are safe?

**8** How can I tell if a follower request is really from a friend?

**9** What does Twitter do with my personal information?

**10** Should I connect my Twitter account to my Facebook account?

# CHAPTER FIVE

# WATCHING OUT FOR ONLINE FRAUD

**T**witter can be a cool way to keep up with friends. It can help you stay current with new trends. However, like other social media, it can be a social disaster. There are thousands of stories of Twitter users embarrassing themselves. However, there are even worse problems than having to repair a reputation. Teen Twitter users have had their accounts hacked. This means that someone illegally accessed accounts on their computer. Cyber crooks may have used malicious software called malware to collect weak passwords. They can then use this stolen data to steal identities.

## Twitter and Cyber Crime

Why are teens at risk of having their Twitter and other social media accounts hacked? How can they protect themselves from online fraud? Teens need to be especially vigilant against cyber crime for several reasons. First, many teens don't have a lot of experience with cyber attacks. They often use easy passwords that they can remember. And they are not always aware of all the different methods

# > HOW BIG IS CYBER CRIME?

The U.S. Federal Bureau of Investigation (FBI) is a leading agency against cyber crime. The FBI takes criminal cyber threats very seriously. According to FBI. gov, cyber crime costs the U.S. economy anywhere from millions to hundreds of billions of dollars every year. However, cyber crime also has implications for national security. According to FBI director Robert Mueller, "Something that looks like an ordinary phishing scam may be an attempt by a terrorist group to raise funding for an operation." He encourages people to do their share in protecting our security. He recommends that everyone use antivirus software on computers and create strong passwords.

FBI director Robert Mueller speaks at the opening of a computer forensics lab in California. Fighting cyber crime has become one of the FBI's top priorities.

that computer criminals can use to gain usernames, passwords, and account information. Teens may not be aware that hackers are trying to phish, spam, and scam them. These thieves want to use teens' computers and accounts, including their Twitter accounts, to illegally make money for themselves. Cyber criminals are smart and often successful.

Twitter is also to blame for some of its users' privacy violations. In 2010, the company settled a complaint from the Federal Trade Commission (FTC). The FTC accused Twitter of failing to safeguard consumers' personal information. In two separate instances, hackers were able to reset Twitter passwords and access private data from users. For example, intruders sent phony messages from Barack Obama. His followers were offered a chance to win $500 in free gas. As a result of these complaints, the FTC is monitoring Twitter more closely. However, this action doesn't mean that Twitter users are safe. In fact, they need to be even more careful about safeguarding their privacy.

## Protect Yourself from Being Phished

There are ways to protect yourself from computer phishing expeditions. Phishing is tricking a user to give up his or her username and password. With this information, computer crooks can gain access to accounts and personal data.

One type of phishing is done through spam. Spam is electronic junk mail that usually tries to sell products or services. If you click on a spam message, it might take you to something that looks like Twitter. Make sure that you are actually on Twitter.com. Cyber criminals have set up Web sites that look a lot like Twitter. However, they have a few changed letters or extra words added. A busy teen might accidentally log in to one of these sites with a username and password. If this has happened to you, you have been phished.

Once crooks have access to your account, they can use it to send spam to your followers and contacts. Cyber criminals might send messages to con Twitter users. They might ask for money to rescue a fake friend who is stranded somewhere without money. Or they might install viruses on your friends' and followers' computers. These viruses can disrupt or destroy software and hardware. All of these are annoying, illegal, and dangerous.

A common way that Twitter users are phished is through direct messages. You might receive a DM from one of your Twitter friends. It invites you to click on a video. Maybe the message claims that it's hilarious and you are in it. When you do click on it, you are taken to Twitter's login page, where you type in your username and password. However, it is not Twitter. And now the crooks have your account information. They may even try to see if you use the same username and password for your other accounts, such as Facebook.

Another video phishing attempt uses a different way to access your computer. When you click on the video that supposedly has you in it, you see a video player. There is a message that asks you to download an update to your video player. However, it is really malware that can gain access to your contacts list. It may even invade the programs on your hard drive. The Internet thieves then send the same phishing DM to all of your followers and names in your different contacts lists. Those who have had this happen will report how embarrassing it is.

# Protect Yourself from Identity Theft

One of the worst things that can happen to you online is someone stealing your identity. This means that an unauthorized person has found your Social Security number, bank information, or credit card numbers. Identity thieves can use this information. They might try to open up credit cards in your name, get student loans, or buy gifts for themselves online.

A 2011 study from ID Analytics estimated that more than 140,000 youths under age eighteen are victims of identity theft each year. College students and young adults ages eighteen to twenty-nine are also prime targets for identity theft. According to a report from the FTC, 31 percent of identity theft victims fall into this age group.

How do you know if your identity has been stolen? Here are some signs: Have you received applications for credit cards all of a sudden? Are you getting direct-mail

ads from stores where you never shop? Has someone called to ask your parents to confirm your employment, even if you haven't applied for a job?

If you do suspect your identity has been stolen, the FTC recommends that you and your parents follow these steps. First, check your credit report from the three nationwide credit reporting companies: Equifax, Experian, and TransUnion. You can request your credit report online, by phone, or through the mail. You can find contact information on the FTC Web site, http://www.ftc.gov. The agency suggests that you file a fraud alert and ask for a credit freeze. This prevents potential thieves from requesting a credit report. You or your parents may also want to file a police report.

## How to Keep Your Twitter Account Safe

Keeping your Twitter account safe means keeping your computer safe. Make sure you have good antivirus and security software installed. Update the software frequently. Do not click on suspicious links. If a link seems weird or odd, it is probably a phishing attempt. For example, if your friends rarely make videos,

licious script detected

Windows Script Host Shell Object

ect

ctivity    RegWrite

Your computer is halted and needs to do someth
about this script.

MsiExec.exe

> Having good antivirus and security software on your computer can help prevent malware from infecting your accounts.

be suspicious about a link to a new video starring you. When using Twitter at school or in a public library, make sure you sign out when you are finished. If you forget, someone else can access your account.

If you think that your account has been hacked or compromised in any way, you should immediately notify Twitter support. Twitter will ask you to create a new password. The company will never ask you to share your old or your new password. If you have received strange DMs from friends, you need to let them know that you are suspicious.

You may want to close your Twitter account. You can open a new account using a new username and password. Make sure that your new username is not your real name. Also make sure that this account is protected.

You don't have to be a victim of online fraud. You have to be on constant guard against attempts to sell you items you don't need or want. Even more important, you need to guard your online identity. Learn about hacking, phishing, and identity theft. Then you can protect your accounts—and yourself—from becoming the next cyber victim.

# STAYING SAFE WHEN USING TWITTER ON YOUR SMARTPHONE

# CHAPTER SIX

Twitter and smartphones seem made for each other. If you are the owner of a smartphone, you can use it to tweet. This makes Twitter easy to use on the fly. Since tweeting from a smartphone is so easy, you need to be even more careful. You may be tempted to tweet without thinking. There are other dangers. Smartphones are mini computers, with the same risks as your home computer. Your accounts can be hacked. Your tweets can carry phishing attempts. Cell phones carry location data that can pinpoint the exact place from which you are tweeting. This can be dangerous. If you lose your smartphone, the finder can try to access your accounts. Good passwords become even more important. Here are some guidelines for staying safe on your smartphone.

## Using Twitter with Your Smartphone

With a smartphone, Twitter users can easily keep their friends updated on their activities wherever they are. Apple

Using Twitter on a smartphone is easy, but teens need to use good decision-making skills to stay safe.

iPhone users and smartphone users with the Android operating system can download Twitter as an app. Then they just need to sign in with their username and password.

Because there is a large risk of losing your phone, secure passwords for all your accounts are essential. A 2012 study by the security company Symantec found that 96 percent of the finders of lost cell phones try to access information on them. Eighty-nine percent of the finders try to open social media apps. Only 50 percent of the people who find a phone try to return it.

According to the Symantec study, barely half of cell phone users password-protect their phones. Phones that don't require a password for access are very vulnerable. Anyone who finds them can instantly use them. A weak password for Twitter will allow anyone to tweet from your account. Can you even imagine what damage that could do?

Smartphone users with many apps might be tempted to use the same password for all of them. This may be convenient. It is also dangerous. This makes it too easy for a cyber thief to access all your accounts. It is much safer to create a strong and different password for each app.

# Protecting Yourself from Spam and Phishing

Smartphone users quickly find out that spam and phishing follow them onto their cell phones. Teens may be particularly at risk of becoming victims on their phones. Teens may be more apt to click on a spam marketer's pitch. Or they may click too quickly on a phishing attempt. They then may give up a password or credit card number to get a money reward. Why do teens do this more than adults?

Spam marketers know how to create ads that tap in to teen emotions. They know how to appeal to teens' desires to be "cool," feel accepted, and appear attractive. A 2009 University of California, Irvine, study showed that when teens feel strong emotions, they tend to make poor decisions. Some of these decisions may result in an angry tweet. Other poor decisions may push teens to agree to an offer for a "free" gift card. Or they may buy items that they don't want or need. These marketing scams rely on the instant response that smartphones allow.

Most teens say that their interactions on social media are mostly positive. However, every teen should be on alert for harassment or bullying.

## Smartphones and Cyberbullying

Smartphones have made cyberbullying on Twitter easier. Teens whose home computers are monitored by parents might be prevented from sending threatening tweets. If they have a smartphone, however, they can send what they want. A 2011 Pew Research Center study revealed that 26 percent of cyberbullying occurred using cell phones.

Smartphone apps have been created to intercept threatening messages. These apps are programmed to flag certain threatening words. They then route the messages to a parent's phone. You can also use the same strategies to fight cyberbullying on your smartphone as you do on your home computer.

## Staying Safe with Location Data

Most teens carry their cell phones with them wherever they go. This was the case with the eighteen-year-old daughter of Michael Dell, head of the computer company Dell, Inc. Wealthy people are often concerned about the kidnapping of themselves and their children. Alexa Dell, however, used her Twitter account to detail her and her parents' exact locations for several weeks in 2012. As soon as Dell's security team found out, her account was closed. You may not be concerned about kidnapping, but you should be concerned about broadcasting your location to the entire Twitter world.

Twitter users can choose to show their location when tweeting. However, this is not the default setting. You should definitely not enable the location setting. While examples of teens being stalked are rare, it does happen. Girls with angry boyfriends, or teens who are fighting, are possibly at risk for being tracked and followed using Twitter. Other apps that you may download for your smartphone should

## > TWITTER ON YOUR > "DUMB" PHONE

It is possible to tweet if you don't have a smartphone. You can post tweets using text messages. First, you have to connect your phone to your Twitter account. Then you can send a tweet by texting it to a phone number called a "short code." While Twitter is free on your phone, text messages are not. Make sure you know your phone carrier's service plan regarding text messages.

clearly inform you about the location data they display. Turning off all location settings will help you stay private.

Staying safe and maintaining your privacy on your smartphone should be a priority. It takes the same knowledge and common sense required to be safe on your home computer. However, you also need to be aware of the particular temptations that cell phones provide. Smartphones allow you almost unlimited access to your social media accounts. You become a constant target for clever marketers. The Global Positioning System (GPS) technology in your cell phone allows Twitter to broadcast your location unless you make sure it is not enabled. And smartphones allow cyberbullies to harass their victims without parental oversight. Staying safe and keeping your smartphone secure takes constant vigilance. However, this caution will pay off as you navigate your technological world with confidence.

# GLOSSARY

**anonymous** Not named or identified.

**antivirus software** Software that is used to prevent, detect, and remove malware and computer viruses.

**app** A software application that is designed to help users accomplish a task.

**avatar** A graphical image that represents a person in cyberspace.

**compromised** Exposed to an unauthorized person.

**default** The preset selection of an option offered by a system, which will always be followed except when deliberately altered.

**harassment** The act of repeatedly irritating or troubling a person with unwelcome behavior; persecution.

**impulsive** Tending to act based on sudden desires, whims, or inclinations, rather than careful thought.

**malicious** Deliberately harmful.

**malware** Software that is used to disrupt computer operation or gather sensitive personal information about the user.

**marketer** A person who is involved in the promotion or selling of goods or services.

**search engine** A computer program that searches the Internet for documents containing keywords specified by the user.

**verify** To confirm the truth of; authenticate.

**vigilant** Keenly watchful to detect trouble or danger.

**vulnerable** Capable of being hurt; open to attack.

Berkman Center for Internet and Society at Harvard University
3 Everett Street, 2nd Floor
Cambridge, MA 02138
(617) 495-754
Web site: http://cyber.law.harvard.edu
The Berkman Center was founded to explore cyberspace,
    share in its study, and help pioneer its development. It
    represents a network of faculty, students, fellows, entre-
    preneurs, lawyers, and virtual architects working to
    identify and engage with the challenges and opportuni-
    ties of cyberspace.

Federal Trade Commission (FTC)
600 Pennsylvania Avenue NW
Washington, DC 20580
(202) 326-2222
Web site: http://www.ftc.gov
This government agency provides resources to learn how
    to deter, detect, and defend against identity theft.

Internet Solutions for Kids, Inc.
1820 E. Garry Avenue, Suite 105
Santa Ana, CA 92705
(877) 302-6858
Web site: http://is4k.com
Internet Solutions for Kids is a nonprofit research organiza-
    tion aimed at understanding the impact on and

opportunities for improving adolescent health repre-
sented by new technologies.

MediaSmarts: Canada's Centre for Digital and Media
   Literacy
950 Gladstone Avenue, Suite 120
Ottawa, ON K1Y 3E6
Canada
(613) 224-7721
Web site: http://mediasmarts.ca
MediaSmarts is a not-for-profit charitable organization for
   digital and media literacy. Its goal is to teach children
   and youth the critical thinking skills they need to engage
   with media as active and informed digital citizens.

National Crime Prevention Council
2001 Jefferson Davis Highway, Suite 901
Arlington, VA 22202
(202) 466-6272
Web site: http://www.ncpc.org
This organization provides explanations, tips, and
   resources for teens who are victims of cyberbullying or
   who want to learn how to prevent it.

StopBullying.gov
U.S. Department of Health & Human Services

200 Independence Avenue SW
Washington, DC 20201
Web site: http://www.stopbullying.gov
This Web site explains what bullying is and what children, teens, and parents can do to prevent it. It offers
  numerous resources to assist teens in dealing with
  cyberbullying and using technology safely.

## Web Sites

Due to the changing nature of Internet links, Rosen Publishing
has developed an online list of Web sites related to the
subject of this book. This site is updated regularly. Please
use this link to access the list:

http://www.rosenlinks.com/21C/Twit

Andrews, Lori. *I Know Who You Are and I Saw What You Did: Social Networks and the Death of Privacy.* New York, NY: Free Press, 2012.

Cross, Mary. *Bloggerati, Twitterati: How Blogs and Twitter Are Transforming Popular Culture.* Santa Barbara, CA: Praeger, 2011.

Diaz-Ortiz, Claire. *Twitter for Good: Change the World One Tweet at a Time.* San Francisco, CA: Jossey-Bass, 2011.

Freedman, Jeri. *Online Safety* (Girls' Health). New York, NY: Rosen Central, 2012.

Hepperman, Christine. *Twitter: The Company and Its Founders* (Technology Pioneers). Minneapolis, MN: ABDO Publishing, 2013.

Ivester, Matt. *lol...OMG! What Every Student Needs to Know About Online Reputation Management, Digital Citizenship, and Cyberbullying.* Reno, NV: Serra Knight Publishing, 2011.

Kamberg, Mary Lane. *Evan Williams, Biz Stone, Jack Dorsey, and Twitter* (Internet Biographies). New York, NY: Rosen Publishing, 2013.

Kiesbye, Stefan. *Are Social Networking Sites Harmful?* (At Issue). Detroit, MI: Greenhaven Press, 2011.

McFedries, Paul. *Twitter: Tips, Tricks, and Tweets.* 2nd ed. Hoboken, NJ: Wiley, 2010.

McQuade, Samuel C., James P. Colt, and Nancy B. B. Meyer. *Cyber Bullying: Protecting Kids and Adults from Online Bullies*. Westport, CT: Praeger Publishers, 2009.

Morris, Tee. *All a Twitter: A Personal and Professional Guide to Social Networking with Twitter*. Indianapolis, IN: Que, 2010.

Obee, Jenna. *Social Networking: The Ultimate Teen Guide* (It Happened to Me). Lanham, MD: Scarecrow Press, 2012.

O'Keeffe, Gwenn Schurgin. *CyberSafe: Protecting and Empowering Kids in the Digital World of Texting, Gaming, and Social Media*. Elk Grove Village, IL: American Academy of Pediatrics, 2011.

O'Reilly, Tim, and Sarah Milstein. *The Twitter Book*. Sebastopol, CA: O'Reilly, 2009.

Rogers, Vanessa. *Cyberbullying: Activities to Help Children and Teens to Stay Safe in a Texting, Twittering, Social Networking World*. Philadelphia, PA: Jessica Kingsley Publishers, 2012.

Wilkinson, Colin. *Twitter and Microblogging: Instant Communication with 140 Characters or Less* (Digital and Information Literacy). New York, NY: Rosen Central, 2012.

Bosker, Bianca. "The Twitter Typo That Exposed Anthony Weiner." HuffingtonPost.com, June 7, 2011. Retrieved September 20, 2012 (http://www.huffingtonpost.com).

Carlson, Nicholas. "The Secret Lives of Teenagers Online: A Full Report from Business Insider." BusinessInsider.com, July 13, 2012. Retrieved August 20, 2012 (http://www.businessinsider.com).

Chang, Juju, and Ely Brown. "KY Teen Sexually Assaulted, Then Threatened with Jail Time." ABC News, August 20, 2012. Retrieved October 1, 2012 (http://abcnews.go.com).

Etherington, Darrell. "Twitter Passes 200M Monthly Active Users, a 42% Increase Over 9 Months." TechCrunch.com, December 18, 2012. Retrieved January 5, 2013 (http://techcrunch.com).

Federal Bureau of Investigation. "Operation Phish Phry: Major Cyber Fraud Takedown." FBI.gov, October 7, 2009. Retrieved September 25, 2012 (http://www.fbi.gov).

Federal Trade Commission. "Children's Online Privacy Protection Act of 1998." FTC.gov. Retrieved September 10, 2012 (http://www.ftc.gov/ogc/coppa1.htm).

Federal Trade Commission. "FTC Testifies on Protecting Teen Privacy." FTC.gov, July 15, 2010. Retrieved September 12, 2012 (http://www.ftc.gov/opa/2010/07/toppa.shtm).

Federal Trade Commission. "Twitter Settles Charges That It Failed to Protect Consumers' Personal Information; Company Will Establish Independently Audited Information Security Program." FTC.gov, June 24, 2010. Retrieved September 12, 2012 (http://www.ftc.gov /opa/2010/06/twitter.shtm).

Ho, Erica. "The 25 Most Popular (and Worst) Passwords of 2011." TIME.com, November 22, 2011. Retrieved August 20, 2012 (http://techland.time.com).

Horn, Leslie. "Teens 'Mostly Kind' on Social Networks, But Bullying Persists." PCMag.com, November 9, 2011. Retrieved July 25, 2012 (http://www.pcmag.com /article2/0,2817,2396099,00.asp).

HuffingtonPost.com. "Fox News Politics Twitter Account Hacked, Disturbing Tweets Appear." July 4, 2011. Retrieved September 3, 2012 (http://www .huffingtonpost.com).

ID Analytics. "More Than 140,000 Children Could Be Victims of Identity Fraud Each Year." July 12, 2011. Retrieved January 5, 2013 (http://www.idanalytics .com/news-and-events/news-releases/2011/7-12 -2011.php).

Lenhart, Amanda. "Cyberbullying 2010: What the Research Tells Us." Pew Internet & American Life Project, May 6, 2010. Retrieved January 6, 2013 (http://www.pewinternet.org).

Lenhart, Amanda, Mary Madden, Aaron Smith, Kristen Purcell, Kathryn Zickuhr, and Lee Rainie. "Teens, Kindness and Cruelty on Social Network Sites." Pew Internet & American Life Project, November 9, 2011. Retrieved July 12, 2012 (http://pewinternet.org).

Leslie, Frances M., Linda J. Levine, Sandra E. Loughlin, and Cornelia Pechmann. "Adolescents' Psychological & Neurobiological Development: Implications for Digital Marketing." Digitalads.org, 2009. Retrieved September 21, 2012 (http://digitalads.org/documents/Leslie_et _al_NPLAN_BMSG_memo.pdf).

Madden, Mary, and Aaron Smith. "Reputation Management and Social Media." Pew Internet & American Life Project, May 26, 2010. Retrieved August 15, 2012 (http:// www.pewinternet.org).

Microsoft Safety & Security Center. "Teach Kids Online Security Basics." 2012. Retrieved August 20, 2012 (http://www.microsoft.com/security/family-safety /childsafety-internet.aspx).

Popkin, Helen A. S. "Getting the Skinny on Twitter's 'Cisco Fatty.'" NBCNews.com, March 27, 2009. Retrieved August 1, 2012 (http://www.msnbc.msn.com).

Richtel, Matt. "Young, in Love and Sharing Everything, Including a Password." New York Times, January 17, 2012. Retrieved July 20, 2012 (http://www .nytimes.com).

Sano, David. "Twitter Creator Jack Dorsey Illuminates the Site's Founding Document." Los Angeles Times, February 18, 2009. Retrieved August 23, 2012 (http://latimesblogs.latimes.com/technology /2009/02/twitter-creator.html).

Snow, Gordon M. "Cybersecurity: Responding to the Threat of Cyber Crime and Terrorism." Federal Bureau of Investigation, April 12, 2011. Retrieved January 5, 2013 (http://www.fbi.gov).

Symantec Corporation. "The Symantec Smartphone Honey Stick Project." 2012. Retrieved October 2, 2012 (http://www.symantec.com/content/en/us/about /presskits/b-symantec-smartphone-honey-stick-project .en-us.pdf).

Vamosi, Robert. "Twitter, a Growing Security Minefield." PCWorld.com, July 22, 2009. Retrieved July 25, 2012 (http://www.pcworld.com).

Vance, Ashlee. "The Very Real Perils of Rich Kids on Social Networks." Bloomberg Businessweek, August 10, 2012. Retrieved September 21, 2012 (http:// www.businessweek.com).

**TWITTER SAFETY AND PRIVACY:**
**A GUIDE TO MICROBLOGGING**

7214

# About the Author

Susan Henneberg, whose previous books for young adults include *Top 10 Tips for Enjoying Success in School*, *Internship Smarts*, and *Money-Making Opportunities for Teens Who Like Working with Kids*, has taught high school and college in Reno, Nevada, for over thirty years. She is inspired by her students and family to stay on top of the latest technology and currently enjoys living in the world of tweets, trends, and hashtags.

# Photo Credits

Cover (figure) infinityPhoto/Shutterstock.com; cover (background), p. 21 © iStockphoto.com/franckreporter; p. 4 Christin Gilbert/age fotostock/SuperStock; p. 7 © Aurora Photos/Alamy; p. 8 © iStockphoto.com/Zmeel Photography; p. 10 Kevin Mazur/WireImage/Getty Images; p. 14 Dougal Waters/Digital Vision/Getty Images; p. 17 Monkey Business Images/Shutterstock.com; pp. 24, 30, 38 © AP Images; pp. 26–27 Wavebreak Media/Thinkstock; p. 32 Brendan Smialowski/Getty Images; pp. 42–43 © iStockphoto.com /Rob Broek; pp. 46–47 © iStockphoto.com/hocus-focus; p. 49 Edyta Pawlowska/Shutterstock.com.

Designer: Michael Moy; Editor: Andrea Sclarow Paskoff; Photo Researcher: Karen Huang